FILE BANKRUPTCY
AND
GET RICH

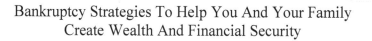

Bankruptcy Strategies To Help You And Your Family
Create Wealth And Financial Security

By Ronald J. Drescher

I hope that reading this book helps you decide to contact our firm and schedule a free consult to talk about your problems and outline a solution. This consult, *a value of over $250*, may help you begin to find financial security, for all the reasons discussed in this book. If you want to skip forward and see why I believe this to be true, read the section discussing my blog, *8 Pieces Of Life Changing Advice A Bankruptcy Lawyer Will Give You For Free* that begins on page 21.

Please don't spend another hour today worrying about what's going to happen tomorrow. Call us at:

(443) 438-1966

We hope to see you soon.

Published by Ronald J. Drescher, Baltimore MD

Printed in the United States of America.

ISBN: ISBN- 13: 978-1530072545

ISBN- 10: 1530072549

Additional copies are available at special quantity discounts for bulk purchases for sales promotions, premiums, fundraising, and educational use.

For more information, please contact: Ronald Drescher, Drescher & Associates, (443) 438-1966
Or visit our website, www.Drescherlaw.com

To find out what other clients have to say about their experience with our firm, visit **DrescherReviews.com**.
Contact the author directly at getrich@drescherlaw.com

We are a debt relief agency. We help people file for bankruptcy relief under the Bankruptcy Code.

Table Of Contents

Introduction

If you're reading this book now, you're struggling. Your car has been repossessed, or you're afraid that it's going to be. Your investment property is worth half what you paid for it, and the bank won't agree to a short sale. You're current on your credit cards, but making the minimum payment every month isn't getting you anywhere. You've stopped answering the phone because caller ID shows you an unfamiliar number and you're worried it's a debt collector.

Clients bring these problems and more into my office every day. Their stories are filled with disheartening episodes of job loss, illness and injury, youthful mistakes, and decisions made after receiving bad or, perhaps worse, no advice. Most clients who invested in real estate still haven't recovered from the downturn of 2008. By the time we meet, they've tried everything: debt consolidation, using cash advances to pay down high rate credit cards, mortgage refinance, failed requests for hardship relief and, worst of all, invading a 401(k) or IRA to pay down bills. Visiting me is usually their last resort.

It's for people like these clients that I created my video series *Why Filing Bankruptcy May Be The Best Thing You Ever Do* (www.bankruptcybestthing.com). In that three part series, I explain how filing bankruptcy will help viewers take control of their lives, understand where the money goes and improve their credit scores. As of May, 2016, over 30,000 people have watched these videos, and hundreds more watch every month. It's my hope that viewers facing money problems can begin to understand that filing bankruptcy can be a catalyst for great change.

Some people believe that bankruptcy is the hard bottom of a terrible fall, but I don't. I see bankruptcy as the beginning of a climb towards a better life, a reconnection with the world and an opportunity for financial security.

When clients come into my office for the first time they're usually filled with fear, anxiety and dread. By the time they leave, most clients tell me that a weight has been lifted off their shoulders and they can sleep at night, often for the first time in years. Knowing I can help these men, women and families overcome their seemingly impossible obstacles drives me to work hard for them. In these pages you'll read a few of the reviews for our firm that satisfied clients have left on Avvo.com, the most popular online lawyer review site.

Building wealth, enjoying financial security and "getting rich" don't happen overnight. Books like *The Millionaire Next Door* and speakers like Dave Ramsey emphasize that enjoying these fruits requires long term planning, disciplined investing, and patience. However, if you're staring up from the bottom of a hole that's been dug for you by hospital bills, old taxes, bad mortgages, and astronomical credit card fees, getting to that good place will be much harder and take much more time. In some cases, your debt may be so debilitating that you'll never be able to get out of the hole without help.

It's for these situations that I wrote this book. You can file bankruptcy and get a jump start to create tremendous prosperity for yourself and your family. In the next chapters I'm going to show you how.

Chapter 1

Build Wealth By Discharging Outrageous Credit Card Debt

Almost every one of my clients has credit card debt.

Getting into trouble with credit cards is easy because the banks

press the cards on us relentlessly. From the instant we graduate

high school we are bombarded with teaser offers for low six month

interest rates that balloon to 18% or higher. While it can feel good

to stay current by making the minimum payments, paying the

credit card balance in that way will take forever.

The table below shows the disclosure from an actual credit

card statement carrying a balance of $13,097.72, and requiring a

minimum payment of $130:

If you make no additional charges using this card and each month you pay...	You will pay off the balance shown on this statement in about...	And you will end up paying an estimated total of...
Only the minimum payment	26 years	$29,392
$458	3 years	$16,482 (Savings=$12,910)

Probably no one reading this will be surprised that repaying the credit card by making only minimum payments will require 26 years. At the end of that time the client will have paid almost $30,000 and have zero dollars in the bank.

If that same client discharged that credit card debt in bankruptcy and invested the same minimum payment, assuming a modest rate of return, the result is vastly different, as shown in this table:

Payment	Term	Rate of Return	Final Value
$130	26 years	4%	**$71,148**

Using this example the client who files bankruptcy and continuously invests the minimum payment will be $71,148 ahead of the client who makes the same payment for 26 years to pay off a high interest credit card. I work through these numbers with my clients during our free initial consults where we look together at the results projected onto a big screen TV in my conference room.

PLANNING WORKSHEET FOR CLIENT CONSULT

When the final savings number comes up I ask, "will having that money in your bank account or IRA make a difference in your life?" With their eyes now wide open, the answer is always "yes".

The results can be even more striking if the debt is higher and the rate of return is higher. Most of my clients have considerably more than $13,000 in credit card debt. If we assume that the debt is twice that, say $25,000, and we apply the standard rate of return that comes up in Google after searching for "rate of return on most conservative mutual fund" (about 6.5%), we get the following results:

Payment	Term	Rate of Return	Final Value
$260	26 years	6.5%	**$210,951.40**

These numbers speak for themselves. By the way, in this last example, a client who decides to skip bankruptcy and pay the minimum payments over 26 years at 18% will have paid the credit card company about $81,126 during that time. Consider this: in one case, a credit card company will have $81,126 of a client's money, while the client will have Zero. In the other case, the credit card company will have Zero while the client will have $210,951.

From 30,000 Feet: Chapter 7 Bankruptcy represents a deal between you and the bankruptcy system.

What you give in bankruptcy

For your part, you will sign papers under penalty of perjury listing your assets, debts, income, expenses, and other items from your financial history. The Chapter 7 trustee (a private lawyer appointed by the government to oversee your case) will decide whether you have equity in your assets, based primarily on what's in your papers, which are called *Schedules*. The trustee knows that you're allowed to keep a certain amount of the equity in your assets depending upon what state you live in. (Equity is the value of your assets less the amount of any liens or mortgages that need to be paid first if that asset is sold.) These are called *exemptions* and I'll discuss them later in Chapter 2.

You meet with the trustee about 30-40 days after you file your bankruptcy case. This meeting is open to creditors (and the public) and the trustee will ask you questions, under oath, about your assets and financial condition. If, after deducting your exemptions, the trustee sees that nothing is left for your creditors, then the trustee will mark that as a *no asset case* and file a *no distribution report* with the bankruptcy court.

This report is not mailed to the debtor, but our office always sends out an email to our clients when that happens, with the subject line **"Good news about your bankruptcy case"**. When this happens, the client is allowed to keep all of the property they want (of course, keeping a home or car with a loan against it requires keeping up the payments). It's a great milestone in Chapter 7 bankruptcy and we like to deliver good news whenever we can. The vast majority of cases filed in the US are such *no asset* cases.

On the other hand, in some states where the exemptions are not especially generous, a debtor's equity in their cash, investments, real estate, furniture and other assets may well exceed the allowed exemptions (this happens frequently when a client has paid off a car that retains significant value). We see this often in Maryland, where exemptions are only $12,000 for a typical case, not including your house and your retirement accounts. Under those circumstances, the Trustee is allowed to sell these assets for the benefit of creditors.

What you get in bankruptcy

The first benefit you get from filing bankruptcy is an *automatic stay* of any act to collect from you. This is a powerful shield that protects you the instant the bankruptcy court receives your filing (which happens immediately by Internet upload). Upon receipt, the court's filing system will issue a case number and you are under the protective umbrella of the federal bankruptcy court.

This automatic stay stops almost every possible act to collect against you dead in its tracks. Lawsuits, garnishments, foreclosures, repossessions, collection calls, negative credit reporting, threatening letters and the like must all cease. It is hard to believe that a force so powerful could be brought into being by the simple act of uploading a bankruptcy petition to the federal court website. Many of my clients experience their first breath of relief in years when I call them or send an email or a text to let them know their case has been filed and the foreclosure sale is canceled.

With the automatic stay in place to maintain the status quo, the bankruptcy case can proceed. This will pave the way for the permanent remedy of bankruptcy: discharge. In exchange for filing honest schedules and cooperating with the trustee, you will receive a discharge of your debts. *Discharge is the legal benefit of being permanently relieved of having to pay a creditor. This is the main reason most people file for bankruptcy.* Presuming that the debtor has been truthful and transparent, in a Chapter 7 bankruptcy the debtor will receive a discharge 60 days after meeting with the trustee. In the absence of fraud or other misdeeds, creditors have no way to defeat that discharge. The debtor can keep his post-bankruptcy income and the exemptions permitted by statute and emerge debt free.

It's the elimination of this crushing debt, and the opportunity to pay yourself instead of your creditors, that creates the ability to build wealth where previously there was none.

Avvo reviews: Nicholas
"Very Happy I Chose Mr. Drescher"

I was extremely pleased in my dealings with Ron. He was easy to work with and is an expert in his field. Most importantly - he took the time to listen to my needs and concerns and came up with the perfect solution for me. Throughout the process he was always available, returning emails and phone calls promptly and always answering my questions. He always treated me as if I was his most important client. Ron is super easy to work with, and he got me great results. I have already referred others to Ron and I

continue to do so.

Chapter 2

Overcome Paralyzing Wage Garnishments

It's unfortunate that the fear of bankruptcy stops many clients from learning about their options before it's too late. Living in fear and denial, the clients allow judgments to be taken against them. Once that happens, creditors can force you to appear in court and disclose where you work, have bank accounts, and list all other assets. Armed with this information, creditors can then seize these assets and, worse yet, begin to garnish wages.

Wage garnishments are perhaps the most debilitating and humiliating problems facing my clients. They are debilitating because they are paid out of after tax income. This means that once you pay withholdings on your total wages to the federal government, the state, Medicare and social security, the creditor will garnish from whatever is left. For clients living paycheck to paycheck, this makes a difficult position impossible.

Having your wages garnished is also humiliating because the creditor is taking your hard earned money and, without legal help, you are powerless to do anything about it.

Under federal and most state laws, creditors can only take 25% of your take home pay. Even so, for most clients, what's left usually isn't enough to pay for the rent or mortgage, the car, groceries, or insurance. To make matters worse, you may want to pay money to a lawyer to solve the problem, but you can't because there's nothing left: the creditor is taking it from you. You don't have enough left over to make payments on even the most lenient of lawyer payment plans. When your wages are being garnished you are working not to improve your life but just to pay off your creditors.

For most clients who can file Chapter 7, the garnishment will stop with either the first or second paycheck after the case is filed. (Sometimes there's a delay in adjusting payrolls, depending upon my client's employer or human resources department. In any event, creditors must return all monies garnished post-bankruptcy.)

The men and women I represent all tell me about the tremendous relief they feel when the garnishment stops and they can start depositing all of their paychecks into their own bank account, instead of the creditor's.

The Chapter 13 Difference

When we analyze client problems, we often compare wage garnishments to Chapter 13 cases for those clients who cannot qualify or will not benefit from a straight Chapter 7 case. They have similarities because both involve making a payment from wages for the benefit of creditors. Here are a few advantages of Chapter 13 over wage garnishments:

- Debtor (that's the person filing bankruptcy) gets credit for all expenses, not just taxes
- Payments continue for 36-60 months, not until the debt is paid; at the end of that time, the debt is discharged, even if not paid in full
- Debtor can ask bankruptcy court to adjust payment if there's a change in circumstances or a hardship

- Payment covers all debts, not just the judgment being garnished

- Non-dischargeable obligations like taxes and domestic support obligations are paid first before credit cards, hospital bills and other general unsecured debts

- May be able to adjust payment amounts based on seasonality of businesses (for example, a landscaper may pay more during the warm weather months and less in the winter)

- May be able in some circumstances to reduce payment by the amount of nondischargeable student loan debts.

The most important factor in this list is that the time period for the payment *will end*: not when the debt is paid but when the Debtor reaches the end of the Chapter 13 plan period, which could be as short as 36 months but never longer than 60 months. At the end of that time the debts are discharged. This advantage becomes most clear when considering the following example, a client who has:

- $50,000 in credit card and hospital bills that have all gone to judgment

- makes $60,000 per year and lives in Maryland

- takes home $42,000 per year/ $3,500 per month

- is single, living alone.

In Maryland, the judgment rate of interest is 10%, which is exorbitant but ironically lower than normal credit card rates exceeding 18%. When wages are garnished, the creditor applies the payments first to interest and then to the judgment balance. So this table shows how long it would take to pay this off in garnishments:

Net Income	25% Garnishment	Total Months	Total Cost of Garnishment
$3,500	$875	78	**$68,176**

In Chapter 13, Debtors pay no interest on the debts paid, even if they've gone to judgment. In this case, because the $60,000 is above the median income for debtors in Maryland (see the table at http://www.justice.gov/ust/means-testing/20151101) there is a 60 month repayment period.

Let's also assume that the debtor's living expenses are allowed at $3,300. This table shows what repayment of this debt would look like in Chapter 13:

Net Income	Chapter 13 Payment	Total Months	Total Cost of Chapter 13
$3,500	$200	60	**$12,000**

Based on these two tables, it would cost the client $56,000 over five years to repay these debts through garnishments. This is a difference of $675 per month. Going back to the example from the first chapter, the following is a table showing the long term benefit of saving and investing this difference:

Payment	Term	Rate of Return	Final Value
$675	15 years	6.5%	**$200,541.00**

The Chapter 7 Recovery of Garnishments

Under the right circumstances the trustee can sue creditors to recover money the debtor paid creditors during the 90 days before bankruptcy. Under this principle, the trustee can also collect money from a creditor who garnished your wages during this time. The good news is that if you have room in your exemptions *you can recover that money for yourself and your family.* This can be a welcome source of cash when you need it the most and it's good to know that the money may not be lost forever.

Exemptions: The Property You Can Keep In Bankruptcy

Whether a trustee will be able to turn assets into cash for creditors depends in part upon *the exemptions* available in that state. Every state allows a debtor to retain some cash, assets, home furnishings, and other property after receiving a discharge from bankruptcy. This retained property constitutes the debtor's exemptions because the assets are exempt from the right of a creditor or trustee to sell the assets and pay claims.

Exemptions differ from state to state. For example, in Maryland most debtors are allowed to keep approximately $12,000 of value in their assets, almost $23,000 of the equity in their home, and all of their qualified retirement accounts. Other assets may also be sheltered.

Sometimes a debtor owns property that is worth more than his allowed exemptions. In that event, the trustee will confront the debtor's attorney with a demand that the debtor turnover the surplus assets for the trustee to sell.

The problem and opportunity of being over exempt

When a client is "over exempt" we try to identify this issue in the planning phase. The client is usually faced with a choice: make payments in Chapter 13 to buy back the surplus equity from creditors over time, or bargain with the Chapter 7 trustee to make a payment (or series of payments) to buy back the equity now.

Many clients simply don't have a choice: with no access to cash, and holding a non-liquid asset, they really have to face the rigors and commitment of a Chapter 13 case. But for many other clients a Chapter 7 asset case is definitely the way to go. This is because the Chapter 7 trustee knows that *the debtor is usually the best buyer for these assets*, and a sale to the debtor, even at a reduced price, beats the unknown question mark of exposing assets to the open market. For this reason, debtors usually can strike a very favorable bargain with the trustee to pay cash to keep their assets. This result is vastly superior to the cost, time commitment, and rigidity of Chapter 13 or, even worse, staying out of bankruptcy and letting the creditors pick away at your assets and your property.

In most cases for the debtor, having to write a check to the trustee is a small price to pay compared to the tens or even hundreds of thousands of dollars in debt that will be discharged in bankruptcy.

Avvo reviews: Chuck
"Couldn't Be Happier"

When I was looking for a bankruptcy attorney for both my ex wife and myself, I thankfully chose Drescher and Associates. Ron and his associates patiently and diligently walked us through the entire process. While bankruptcy can be stressful, Ron instilled confidence in us throughout the entire process. I couldn't be happier about my decision to choose Ron and his staff and give my highest recommendation to anyone considering enlisting his firm.

Chapter 3

Financial Ruin: Invading Individual Retirement Accounts

The perceived stigma of public shaming that debtors fear from bankruptcy can be so great that clients will make ruinous decisions about their own financial health. The worst decision you could make? Invading a retirement account to pay dischargeable debts.

I wrote a blog item called 8 Pieces Of Life Changing Advice A Bankruptcy Lawyer Will Give You For Free. The blog was intended as a call to action for distressed debtors to seek legal advice, usually given for free, from a bankruptcy lawyer. One of the most important points I emphasized was that "Without paying a dime a client will learn that ... they should not invade their IRA or 401(k)". When I wrote this, I stressed that if this free advice was followed it could change the course of lives, families *and even generations.*

Was this just a puff piece? I didn't think so then and I don't think so now, especially with the explosive growth in the equities markets since that blog's publication in July, 2012. The real truth is that if a family has $100,000 in a protected retirement account when the parents are, say, 45 years old, that money can grow tax free until withdrawals become forced at the age of 70. So if the money grows at 4%, the value in 25 years will be $266,583.63. If the money grows at 7% the value will be $542,743.26. (Source? Future Value Calculator, http://www.investopedia.com/calculator/fvcal.aspx).

Let's get back to the 45 year old parents with $100,000 in an IRA. They may have income interruption, bills to pay, a struggling business. Do they invade the IRA or consider bankruptcy? If they invade the IRA and spend the $100,000 they will incur a 10% penalty (usually withheld upon an early withdrawal) and then the rest of the $100,000 goes immediately into taxable income, probably forcing the client into a higher tax bracket. If the taxes aren't paid then and there, the unpaid tax liability (and the interest on the taxes) will become nondischargeable in bankruptcy, compelling the client into an installment plan with the IRS over several years.

When this happens the balance sheet of the family will become very ugly.

Can they recover in 25 years? Perhaps. *If not, then the family will be left not only without the $542,000 they may have had, but also without the extra money the IRS will grab in the years to come after the decision was made to invade the retirement account.* This money could have been added to the IRA or 401(k) and further increased the family's net worth, significantly affecting the family for a very long time.

Frequently Asked Question: I Have A Little Extra Cash, Should I Make An IRA Contribution Before I File Bankruptcy?

The answer to this question is not very clear, because there are many factors that go into whether or not making a contribution to your IRA on the eve of your bankruptcy case is a transaction done in good faith. Typically you are allowed to perform what's called **pre-bankruptcy planning** before filing your bankruptcy case. This involves arranging your affairs so that you pay as little as possible to the trustee after you file bankruptcy. The concern when you make an IRA contribution is that you're taking money that would have been available to pay creditors and putting it into a retirement account. IRAs are almost universally considered to be exempt assets that the trustee and creditors can't reach.

Nevertheless, the bankruptcy court usually permits this type of planning. However, if there's a perception that a debtor has been too aggressive in spending their cash or rearranging their assets before they file bankruptcy, the court could find that the filing was in bad faith, or the exemption is denied. In the worst case scenario, the discharge will be lost because you transferred assets within a year before the bankruptcy, with an intent to hinder, defeat or delay your creditors. If that happens, it will likely be a problem without a solution. Proper pre-bankruptcy planning is a subtle and sensitive process, and if it's not handled property the results could be disastrous.

Avvo review: Brian
"Ron Drescher Helped Me Start Life Over Again"

Because of the perfect storm of a divorce, the real estate crash (eventual foreclosure on a million dollar house) and an untimely downturn in my business, I accumulated significant personal debt that I couldn't resolve.

Ron Drescher was recommended by my accountant.

When I first met Ron, his friendly and comfortable manner instantly put me at ease. He helped me understand my situation from a non-emotional perspective, and also helped me feel less like a heel for having to consider bankruptcy in the first place.

Ron successfully guided me through the bankruptcy process, and I was eventually granted a compete discharge while still getting to keep the few assets that I have that are important to me, including my interest in my own business.

Lastly, compared to the cost of other bankruptcy lawyers in my area, Ron offered his services for a fair price that I was able to manage.

I would highly recommend Ron Drescher!

Chapter 4

Discharge Income Taxes Instead of Requesting an Offer in Compromise

Most people know the general rule that income tax debts are not dischargeable in bankruptcy. What they may not know is that if six elements are present, these taxes ARE discharged. There are three timing and three non-timing elements.

The timing elements

1. Taxes must be three years old as of the date of filing bankruptcy, with the key date being the first date that tax returns become due (i.e., April 15 of the year following the tax year in question unless you obtained an extension until October 15);

2. Returns must have been filed at least two years before the bankruptcy; and

3. Taxes must have been assessed at least 240 days before the bankruptcy.

The no-timing elements

4. If taxes were assessable pre-bankruptcy, but not assessed until after bankruptcy, they will not be discharged;

5. Returns must not have been tainted by fraud; and

6. Taxpayer must not have engaged in willful tax evasion.

In practice, unless there are unusual circumstances, if the timing elements have been met the taxes will be dischargeable.

Clients often come to me after years of frustration dealing with the IRS. Attempts to get out from under crippling tax debt are often defeated when the collection agent finds that the taxpayer is still young enough to repay a greater portion of the tax than proposed. Sometimes the IRS will sit on offers for months or years.

The ability to discharge moderately old tax debts in bankruptcy usually comes as a delightful surprise to my clients, who have been told that they must live with the taxes for ten years while the IRS levies, garnishes and seizes their income and their assets.

Consulting with a tax advisor is always recommended: after all, knowledge is power. Still, taxpayers should at the same time explore the ability to discharge tens or hundreds of thousands of dollars of income tax (or more) by a single process of filing bankruptcy.

Tax Success: Earl's Story
"Honest, upfront and no games"

Earl came to me with nearly $500,000 in past due taxes. I was not his first consult. Every other lawyer he talked to advised that back taxes are not dischargeable in bankruptcy. Fortunately for Earl, he did not stop his search for the correct advice. He found our firm and here's his experience, in his own words:

I hired Ron for a tricky bankruptcy with close to a half a million dollars in tax liens. After countless attorneys telling me it could not be done, I now have in my possession not only a clean discharge (my credit reports show zero past due accounts) but I also have documentation from both the state and the IRS that all liens have been released and they consider them to be discharged.

My advice: Hire Ron, give him what he needs, and go back to living your life. He knows what he is doing.

Chapter 5

Restructure Car Loans in Chapter 13

Anyone who wants to see the most egregious forms of predatory lending should take a look car loans made to borrowers with bad credit. Interest rates skyrocket over ten percent, forcing the term of the loan into six or seven years or longer. Lenders also roll loans from trade-in vehicles worth less than the loans against them, so by the time the client drives their new car off the lot the vehicle is encumbered by loans significantly exceeding its value.

Chapter 13 allows borrowers to "cram down" the amount of the loan to the value of the vehicle, but only for those cars that the debtor has owned for 910 days (about 2 ½ years). Cram down is a bankruptcy concept that means a secured loan can be restructured to the debtor's advantage, frequently against the will of the creditor. This can offer tremendous savings.

Let's assume a car loan of $26,000 securing a vehicle with a value of $19,000. The payment is $640 and the interest rate is 8.5%. This payment becomes a burden that will tempt the client to file Chapter 7 and surrender the vehicle, with the hope that they can get a cheaper car after bankruptcy or just hold onto the car and discharge the remainder of their debt. But this plan usually doesn't work out well, because the car loan may be itself a source of the client's financial distress, or the cost of getting into another car may be prohibitively expensive. This makes the Chapter 13 restructure option well worth considering

As long as the client has owned the car for 910 days, in Chapter 13 the debtor can restructure the payment by reducing the principal balance to the car's value, dropping the interest rate to a reasonable 5% and paying the loan over 60 months. The before and after picture would look like this:

Before:

Principal	Interest	**Payment**	Term	Total Payments
$26,000	8.5%	**$640**	48 months	$30,761.08

After:

Principal	Interest	**Payment**	Term	Total Payments
$19,000	5%	**$358**	60 months	$21,480

Besides saving money on the total payments, the reduction of the payment significantly increases the affordability of the car and reduces the cash flow pressures on the client.

Avvo review: John
"A Very Smart, Aggressive Lawyer With Great Integrity"

Ron is one of the most knowledgeable bankruptcy and debt attorneys I know. He is certainly in the top five in the Maryland area. I have known Ron for over 15 years and have used Ron's services in the past. I had a terrible experience with another attorney in the same practice area and then was introduced to Ron by a business associate. Ron tells you what you need to hear not necessarily what you want to hear as far as advice but I've never gone wrong following his advice. I would recommend him to you if you need an attorney in his practice area. I always refer Ron to anyone needing a bankruptcy or debt lawyer. My referrals have always been pleased.

Chapter 6

Cramdown Investment Properties in Chapter 11

Since the real estate downturn in 2008 investors have faced

the difficult choice of trying to salvage or abandon their investment

properties. Until that time, investors had relied upon the steady

increase in property values to raise cash through loan refinancing.

After values plummeted that source of cash dried up.

Without that cash, landlords had increased pressure

maintaining the properties in the face of vacancies, tenant defaults,

and normal repair expenses. Without sufficient rents and reserves

landlords frequently became delinquent on the mortgages securing

the investment properties. When lenders begin the foreclosure

process, property owners need to decide whether to try and keep

the properties or let them go. One option to obtain long term relief

is Chapter 11 bankruptcy.

Chapter 11 is a flexible procedure that allows businesses

(and individuals with sophisticated financial situations) the opportunity to restructure or reorganize their finances. The central document in Chapter 11 is the Plan of Reorganization, which is the blueprint that a debtor presents to creditors and the Bankruptcy Court. In the Plan, the debtor explains how they intend to treat each class of claims.

In Chapter 11, a debtor is permitted to ask the court to restructure secured debt by reducing the principal balance to the value of the property; reducing the interest rate to a market rate of interest; or extending the term of the obligation. This is similar to the Chapter 13 treatment of automobiles discussed in the previous chapter, but on a larger scale. What's important is that while Chapter 13 plans are limited to 60 months, Chapter 11 plans may extend payments over a much longer term, even up to 30 years.

Common in Chapter 11 is a scenario where investment property has declined in value to, for example, $400,000, but the liens against the property may be as much as $550,000. Bankruptcy Courts have the power to restructure this obligation, even if it's been several years since the investor made any payments to the lender. A typical repayment plan could look something like this:

- Term: 360 months

- Interest rate: 5%

- Principal: $400,000

- Payment: $2,147.29

If the investor is able to rent the property for enough to pay the new debt service then all of the appreciation in the property will belong to the investor, not the lender. This result can immediately rehabilitate an investment that had lost all of its value.

Similarly, in both Chapter 11 and Chapter 13, liens that are completely underwater (where more is owed than the worth of the property) may be stripped off, allowing the owner to clear title and capture all future appreciation. Using the example above, let's assume that during the height of the real estate boom the investor obtained a second mortgage for $50,000 in the property, junior to the original $550,000 loan. By using the tools available in Chapter 11, in addition to reducing the principal balance to $400,000, the value of the property, the investor can now completely remove the junior lien.

Frequently Asked Question: Can an Individual File for Chapter 11?

If you can't quality for Chapter 7 or 13, you may still get bankruptcy relief under Chapter 11. Why would you need to do that?

If your income is too high and you don't have sufficient deductions, you're probably going to be forced out of Chapter 7 by *the means test*. This is a test that determines whether a debtor who owes primarily consumer debts has sufficient means to repay some of their debt. The focus of the bankruptcy court is on the debtor's household income. If this income is over the median income of that debtor's state, there is a risk that the debtor won't qualify to discharge all of their debts in Chapter 7. (For example, as of 2016 the median income in Maryland for an individual debtor is just under $60,000, and for a family of four is approximately $107,000. Maryland, however, is one of the highest median income states.) If the debtor doesn't qualify for a complete discharge in Chapter 7, the next question is, can the debtor file for Chapter 13?

Chapter 13 is a procedure for debtors to obtain a discharge over a period of three to five years by making monthly payments to a Chapter 13 trustee. This trustee, unlike a Chapter 7 trustee, doesn't have the power to sell your assets; a Chapter 13 trustee is really an administrator who reviews proposed payment plans and, once approved, collects the debtor's payments and pays out to creditors. After all the payments are made, the debtor receives the same discharge she would have received immediately in Chapter 7.

Chapter 13, however, is not available to everyone. If a debtor owes too much of either secured debt (like a home mortgage or a car payment) or unsecured debt (like credit cards, taxes and student loans), then the debtor won't qualify for Chapter 13. These debt limits fluctuate from year to year based on the cost of living, but they are set by statute and they are rigidly enforced (as of 2016, for unsecured debt, the limit is about $385,000; for secured debt, about $1,100,000).

If you don't qualify under the debt limits for Chapter 13,

and your gross income is too high for Chapter 7, you won't necessarily be deprived of relief under the bankruptcy laws, because you might qualify for Chapter 11. Chapter 11 is a procedure for businesses, but also for high-income individuals with a fairly sophisticated financial situation, who want or need to file their own plan of reorganization to reorder their financial affairs. Under Chapter 11, the debtor proposes their own plan, and creditors have a right to vote to accept or reject the proposal. If the plan succeeds, the treatment the debtor promises under the *plan of reorganization* substitutes the debts the debtor owed when they filed bankruptcy. Chapter 11 is a much more flexible process than Chapter 13.

Avvo review: Martha
"At Last, The Banks Could Not Ignore Me Anymore…"

Since 2008 when the financial crisis hit us, I had been struggling, trying to keep 3 of the investment properties I had acquired to create cash flow for my retirement. After a successful career as a real estate broker and investor, I lost my job and went through a very difficult divorce. I contacted the mortgage holders and asked for some time to find a new job and to start producing again. However, I received no help. Instead, I was told that the information and documents (I KNEW I HAD SENT) had not been received or, I was just ignored ... Everybody advised me just to forget about those properties. But I knew how hard how hard it would be to acquire similar properties with my current credit worthiness and I knew how hard I had worked to buy and keep them for so many years. I wanted to save my properties. Everybody aware of my situation advised me just to forget about those properties but, good thing, I did not listen. Instead, I kept on asking and researching for help.

Finally, one day, I found a video clip on youtube where Mr. Drescher explained how to prepare the "Disclosure" and the "Plan" for a Chapter 11 Bankruptcy. (The value of my properties was over the limit to file for the Chapter 13 reorganization). I decided to call the number and I was very surprised when Mr. Drescher answered the phone himself. He explained the process step by step and, thanks to his knowledge and experience, I just received the confirmation of my plan. My loans were restructured and I will be able to start making the mortgage payments again and kept my properties. Thanks Mr. Drescher!

Chapter 7

Walk Away From Your Underwater House And Save A Fortune

My clients frequently resort to extreme efforts to save their homes. Devoting frequently more than half their disposable income to service an overpriced mortgage, these clients cannot overcome a deep emotional attachment to their residence. They are frustrated by the years spent in a fruitless effort to obtain a loan modification. During this time many months and even years will pass with lenders refusing to accept payments but still not foreclosing, creating deeper and deeper holes for the client to climb out of in the hope of staying in their home.

By the time the last loan modification is denied, my clients have only the option of filing Chapter 13, resuming normal mortgage payments and curing the delinquency, with interest, usually over 60 months. Although this is usually their last, best hope to save their home, the real cost of choosing this option is often devastating.

The problem is that loans secured solely by a debtor's principal residence cannot be modified in bankruptcy. Thus unlike the strategies discussed in the last chapter about cramming down a lien on investment property, the home mortgage must remain as written in the contract.

The terrible impact of fighting to save these homes can be clearly seen from a review of the numbers. If we assume a home with a $500,000 thirty year fixed mortgage accruing interest at 7.5%, the monthly payment would be $3,496.07. If the borrower hasn't made a payment in two years, total arrears would be $83,905 (more if attorney's fees and other costs of collection are included). The cure payment on this in Chapter 13 (assuming an interest on the cure of 5%) would be *$1,583.39*. Since the borrower needs to resume normal monthly payments the total monthly cost of retaining the home is *$5,079.46*.

This figure becomes especially alarming if the value of the home has dropped significantly below the amount of the mortgage (which is often the case), with little or no hope that the borrower will ever build any real equity in the residence. In this case the homeowners are really paying ***exorbitant rent.***

If the borrower can manage to find and rent a home with half that rent, and file bankruptcy to discharge their personal liability on the mortgage, then over 60 months the net savings will look like this:

Monthly Savings	No. of months Invested at 6.5%	Total Savings
$2,500	60	**$176,684.92**

While clients frequently have a difficult time accepting the real family value of letting go of their residence, the monumental benefits of making this decision are inescapable.

Avvo review: Spencer
"A Source Of Calm And Confidence Through Difficult Times"

Ron Drescher's confidence and command of bankruptcy law and process was the lighthouse that guided us through the most difficult financial time in our lives.

Faced with an overwhelming business and personal situation, Ron rolled up his sleeves, executed pin-point research, and made quick, correct recommendations. He firmly and fairly dealt with the myriad of vendors and creditors in our very complicated situation. When appropriate, he treated them with the same respectful and compassionate manner I would have wanted to if I was able. At the same time, he defended our rights, did not let anyone take advantage of us, and shutdown unfair claims being made by large creditors with significant legal departments behind them.

The anxiety created by the difficult decisions we had to make, and the unknown consequences resulting from them were our biggest fear. Ron always weighed the potential outcomes and gave us the various options we had available to us. His clear and calm explanation always put us at ease and gave us the bit of confidence we needed to make difficult decisions.

Finally -- Ron's fees are absolutely fair and we were never surprised by an invoice we received from him. He gave us accurate estimates of costs up front and did not waiver from that cost unless there was a clear change in scope.

If you are in the position where you are looking for bankruptcy services - Ron Drescher is the professional that will put you at ease. Making the decision to do this is the toughest part. Once you have made that decision - Ron will take the burden off your shoulders and move you through the process efficiently. All of that being said, the best thing we can say is that Ron treated us with sympathy and respect when very few people would. He brings more than a simple attorney-client relationship to the experience and we appreciated his genuine care for our welfare.

Chapter 8

Redeem Personal Property In Chapter 7

In Chapter 5 I talked about the benefits of restructuring car loans in Chapter 13. Under the right circumstances, this benefit is also available in Chapter 7 under the concept of *redemption*.

Redemption of personal property happens when property, usually a car, is subject to a lien and the amount owed is significantly higher than the value of the car. If the debtor has access to enough cash, the debtor can make a one-time cash payment to the lender and own the car free and clear of the lender's claim. Perhaps the money comes from a relative, or a 401(k) loan or from the debtor's other exemptions. So if a car is worth $8,000 but secures an obligation of $15,000, a single payment of $8,000 will force the lender to release its lien on the vehicle.

The obvious disadvantage of doing this in Chapter 7 instead of Chapter 13 is that the client needs to come up with all of the money at one time, instead of over 60 months of payments.

However, the major advantage is that the debtor does not need to have owned the car for 910 days: they can make the redemption at any time once the Chapter 7 case is filed.

Avvo review: Mi Mi
"What A Peaceful And Stressfree Experience"

From the moment I began speaking with Mr. Drescher about my personal financial situation, I knew that I didn't make a mistake by contacting his firm. I was definitely nervous at first but Mr. Drescher took the time to FULLY educate me on the entire process and gave the very best advice and suggestions to ultimately achieve a favorable outcome for me. Mr. Drescher and his team of professionals were caring, understanding and compassionate from beginning to end. They responded timely and addressed all of my questions and concerns, as well as keeping me informed of updates and changes. Although making the decision to file was scary at first, Mr. Drescher displayed the confidence that I needed to see in order to completely trust and believe in his firm. My bankruptcy ordeal was a breeze and I was so grateful to have his guidance every step of the way. I now have a successful closed

case and I am truly thankful for my fresh start.

Chapter 9

The Bankruptcy Miracle:
Improve Your Credit Score

This is what happened to Earl, my client from Chapter 4 who had half a million dollars in tax debts discharged after bankruptcy. Two years after his discharge, Earl wrote me this very encouraging email:

All 3 scores mid 7s. Not one lien shows on any bureau. 23 months out of BK and just got approved. Not qualified, but flat out thru underwriting approved for a house. They say to never forget those who helped you along the way, so thanks again for your professionalism and honesty in an occupation where those two words are seldom associated with one another.

I spend time in almost every consult talking about how filing bankruptcy will impact my client's credit score. The issue usually comes up when the client asks "how long will the bankruptcy stay on my credit report?" Here's the truth: according to the credit reporting company Experian, a Chapter 7 bankruptcy stays on your credit report for up to 10 years. There's no denying that filing bankruptcy is a blemish on your credit report. But that's not the whole story.

A credit report is a dynamic, changing document. In computing a credit score, recent events are given greater weight, as a bad credit history does fade into the background as time goes by. Creditors report delinquent payments, lawsuits, judgments and charge-offs regularly, and your credit score will suffer every time these mishaps get reported. On the other hand, your score improves when creditors report that you are timely repaying your car loan, home mortgage or credit card balance.

For every client, we order a comprehensive credit report to help them get their bearings and identify creditors. These reports also give a projection of what clients can expect to happen to their credit reports after bankruptcy. This image shows how dramatically scores usually improve very soon after bankruptcy:

Credit Score Analysis

Current Score	12 Month Post-bankruptcy Credit Score	Net Credit Score Effect
488	642	+154
477	598	+121
535	652	+117

Certainly every case is different and to be sure, sometimes credit scores will go down, but for the most part a credit score will enjoy an increase after filing for bankruptcy. I recently spoke with a client whose score improved from 480 to over 600 after filing bankruptcy *and hasn't even received his discharge yet!*

Why are credit scores important?

Your credit score is a dominant factor in determining both whether you get a loan and, if you do, how much that loan will cost. A person with a good credit score may pay as much as 10% lower on borrowed money than a person with a worse score.

Over time and given a large enough amount of a loan, the difference can be significant. On a home loan of $400,000, here is the difference in interest over the thirty year life of a loan between a person paying 4% fixed interest and a person paying 7%:

Rate	Payment	Total Interest Paid
4%	$1,910	$287,478
7%	$2,661	$558,036

This difference results in a payment that is $750 per month higher and will cost almost $270,000 more over the life of the loan. Having a better credit score can mean enormous savings to a borrower and their family.

Looking at the numbers from a different perspective, having a good credit score can increase a borrower's *spending power*. In the above example, the borrower with the better credit score gets a $400,000 loan paying $1,910 per month, while the other borrower has to pay $2,661. If the borrower with the good credit score could afford to pay $2,661 and get the money at only 4% (instead of 7%), then they might qualify for a loan of $557,376.36, $150,000 more than the borrower who must pay 7%.

This is a huge difference that could change the entire life of a family. It could allow them to buy into a good neighborhood, with safer streets and better schools. No one can put a price tag on these benefits.

Why does your Credit Score go up After Bankruptcy?

After you receive a bankruptcy discharge, creditors MUST stop making any efforts to collect the discharged debt. This law is supported by the *discharge injunction*, a powerful federal shield that protects debtors from creditors and allows them to enjoy a fresh start. Creditors simply aren't allowed to take any action that would be an effort to collect the debt. But bear in mind that the discharge injunction may not legally prevent the creditor from reporting your payment history.

Post-bankruptcy, creditors are technically allowed to continue to report that claims are delinquent on their borrowers' credit reports. This is not against the law. However, **creditors are regularly sued** when they fail to report these claims as "discharged in bankruptcy". Almost any other reporting can be seen as a violation of the discharge injunction.

Creditors have come to learn that if they continue to report that a debt is due and owing or delinquent, that creditor runs the risk that the debtor will file a lawsuit against the creditor. It will then be up to the creditor to convince the court that the reporting was not an effort to collect that discharged debt. Creditors don't want the risk and expense that comes with defending a lawsuit. They almost all follow the practice of reporting bad debts as discharged and then leaving them alone.

This is good news for my clients. After filing bankruptcy, the most recent reporting to the credit bureaus is usually that the debtors *are current*: on their car loans or the new, secured credit card they received after bankruptcy. This means that credit scores tend to go up, not down, for most people who were seriously delinquent on their debts before filing bankruptcy.

For other people, who have struggled heroically to remain current on their suffocating debt for months or even years, their good credit scores are typically restored within two years after filing, if they maintain good debt practices after bankruptcy. Scores in the 700's are not unusual for clients who pursue their fresh start as a meaningful opportunity to bring real change to their lives.

Conclusion

I spoke with a trustee recently who marveled that there is no faster way to improve your net worth than to file bankruptcy. Will filing make you rich? No, not without some additional work on your part. I wrote this book to give you a head start.

This book is based on the power of compounding, a well-known secret in the world of finance and investing. When money is invested over a long period of time, the results can be impressive. On the other hand, the single greatest threat to successful investing is not choosing bad stocks, bonds and mutual funds, but rather being mired in debt.

In this book, I tried to show how bankruptcy can do more than just give you peace of mind and protection from creditors: it can be the first step on the road to wealth and financial security. If you're wondering how it can help you, please contact us: we'd love to hear from you.

Ronald J. Drescher
Drescher & Associates, P.A
4 Reservoir Circle, Suite 107
Baltimore, MD 21208
Telephone (443) 438-1966; Fax (410) 484-8120

Delaware Office - 1 Commerce Center
1201 North Orange Street, Suite 722
Wilmington, Delaware 19801
Rondrescher@Drescherlaw.com
http://www.Drescherlaw.com
MDBankruptcyLawyer – YouTube

Made in the USA
Middletown, DE
21 January 2017